Henry W. Acland

The Inaugural Robert Boyle Lecture

Founded by the Oxford University Junior Scientific Club in May, 1892

Henry W. Acland

The Inaugural Robert Boyle Lecture
Founded by the Oxford University Junior Scientific Club in May, 1892

ISBN/EAN: 9783337036508

Printed in Europe, USA, Canada, Australia, Japan

Cover: Foto ©ninafisch / pixelio.de

More available books at **www.hansebooks.com**

THE INAUGURAL

ROBERT BOYLE LECTURE

FOUNDED BY THE

Oxford University Junior Scientific Club

IN MAY, 1892

BY

SIR HENRY W. ACLAND, BART.

K.C.B., F.R.S.

REGIUS PROFESSOR OF MEDICINE IN THE UNIVERSITY OF OXFORD
HONORARY STUDENT OF CHRIST CHURCH
FORMERLY LEE'S READER IN ANATOMY

Oxford: 116 High Street

LONDON: HENRY FROWDE, AMEN CORNER, E.C.

1892

TO THE

OXFORD UNIVERSITY JUNIOR SCIENTIFIC CLUB

AND TO ALL

WHO FOLLOW IN THE STEPS OF

ROBERT BOYLE

INAUGURAL ADDRESS

Mr. President,

The occasion of the present gathering is to inaugurate the Lecture which the Oxford University Junior Scientific Club has now founded.

You, Mr. President, have stated the reasons which induced your Society to take this important step, and I have only in this regard to inform your guests how it has come about that I should presume to address such an audience on so great an occasion.

You decided to found a periodical Lecture, and to name it after Robert Boyle. It was natural and proper, this being so, that you should ask the present President of the Royal Society to be the first to address you. Lord Kelvin, by reason of many and weighty engagements to which he was pledged, was forced to decline. That you should lose Lord Kelvin, or, as I hope, only have his presence delayed for a time, was deeply to be regretted. His predecessor in his great office, Sir George Gabriel Stokes, having added to his professorial and parliamentary duties the onerous task of delivering this term a course of the Gifford Lectures in Edinburgh, found it also quite impossible now to come.

Though it might seem to place me in a false position before you and the world to attempt to supply the place of Lord Kelvin or Sir Gabriel Stokes, yet when pressed by your officers I could not refuse. The least capable, in many respects, of the scientific staff, I yet felt my young friends had a right to the service of the oldest of that staff, should they seriously desire it. I therefore endeavour to stop the gap, as I hope, for Lord Kelvin and Sir Gabriel Stokes until other years.

Then came the difficult task of selecting under these circumstances the subject of my discourse. After much consideration I have decided to describe, as well as I am able in the brief space of an Address, the place in Science and the character of Robert Boyle ; and then to ask your Society and the University, are you willing, firstly, two centuries after his death in 1691, to hold him up as a conspicuous example of an Oxford scientific man, and secondly, will the means now at your disposal enable you to follow in his steps ?

ROBERT BOYLE, seventh son of the 1st Earl of Cork, was born in 1626, at Lismore in County Waterford, the year after the death of Bacon. He left Ireland at the age of eight in a gale of wind, and when the coast was 'infested by the Turkish Gallies'; but, after touching at ' Ilfordcombe and Minehead' he happily arrived at Bristol. He shortly afterwards went to Eton, where (we are told) 'he lost much of that Latin he had got ; for he was so addicted to the more solid parts of knowledge that he hated the study of bare words naturally.' Such was his biographer's view of the respective merits of rival systems of education.

In 1638 he proceeded to the Continent, passing through Normandy to Paris, thence to Lyons, and thence to Geneva, where he stayed twenty-one months. During his residence abroad he learnt the language so completely, as to pass, when he thought fit, for a Frenchman. All he did he did thoroughly, thereby setting an example that will never be out of date.

He went on to Florence, where, in his own words, ' he spent his spare hours in reading . . . the new paradoxes of that great stargazer Galileo,' whose ' ingenious books (he relates), perhaps because they could not be so otherwise, were confuted by a decree from *Rome* ; his highness the Pope, it seems, presuming, and that justly, that the infallibility of his chair extended equally to determine points in philosophy and in religion, and loth to have the stability of that earth questioned, in which he had established his kingdom [1].'

At length Boyle arrived at Rome, where he passed as a Frenchman. He was shocked by much which he saw and heard of the life and immorality of even the Clergy there. He studied unceasingly, reading much on all his journeys. He returned to London in 1646, where he fell into the company of what he calls the 'Invisible College,' that is, the body which afterwards became the Royal Society. In 1648 'some of us removed to Oxford,' when Dr. Wilkins, Dr. Goddard, Dr. Ward, Dr. Bathurst, Dr. Willis, and others, met in an apothecary's house, and afterwards in Dr. Wilkins' lodgings in Wadham College.

The course of Boyle's life must be considered as now fully determined. He had gradually acquired a keen interest both in Science and Theology, an interest never to be abated, and henceforth interlaced with all his thoughts and writings.

Shortly after his return to England, in 1644, he had, with the 'Invisible College,' devoted himself to chemical enquiries and experiments. These engrossing

[1] Boyle's Works, vol. i. xxiv.

pursuits were interrupted by a visit to Ireland in 1652. There he made anatomical dissections with Sir William Petty, verifying by actual experiment the circulation of the blood, by the discovery of which Harvey had changed the whole course of Physiological science.

In 1654 he came to live in Oxford. There, partly in the lodgings of the Warden of Wadham, and partly in his own rooms near University College, he engaged in regular scientific experiments. Hooke, whose name Sir John Herschel justly mentions with honour, was employed by him.

After a time he removed to London, in 1668, and thenceforward was in constant intercourse with the Fellows of the now fully established Royal Society. He was one of its first Council, but in 1680, from certain scruples, declined the office of President, which was then accepted by Sir Christopher Wren.

Among his friends were to be reckoned Newton, Locke, Sydenham, Wallis, and Wren, for some time also Spinoza, and for many years Bishop Burnet.

His services to Science are summed up by an accomplished writer of his life in the National Biography, as 'unique, notwithstanding occasional failing on the side of credulousness'; if so, this was a failing which he shared in common with

Bacon. It was due rather to the age than to the person.

'The condition of his birth, the elevation of his character, the engrossing enthusiasm of his researches, combined to lend dignity and currency to their results. These were coextensive with the whole range of experimental investigation then accessible. He personified, it might be said, in a manner at once impressive and conciliatory, the victorious revolt against scientific dogmatism then in progress. Hence his unrivalled popularity and privileged position, which even the most rancorous felt compelled to respect.' ' He was considered (we read) to have inherited, nay outshone, the fame of the great Verulam.' On the side of Literature, Addison cites his work in several papers of the Spectator, and in one mentions him with almost extravagant praise, as 'an honour to his country and a more diligent as well as successful enquirer into the works of Nature than any other nation has ever produced.' On the side of Science, the celebrated Boerhaave declares that ' to him we owe the secrets of fire, air, water, animals, vegetables, fossils ; so that from his works may be deduced the whole system of material knowledge [1].'

[1] See specially Weld's History of the Royal Society ; Dr. Birch's Life of Boyle, and his edition of Boyle's works ; Dr. Peter Shaw's

These praises may sound excessive; and in our days Sir John Herschel indeed speaks of him with somewhat scant praise. 'Boyle,' he says, 'seemed animated by an enthusiasm of ardour, which hurried him from subject to subject and from experiment to experiment without a moment's intermission, and with a sort of undistinguishing appetite.'

This may possibly be correct. But it gives to a casual reader no true impression of his real industry and power. During Boyle's lifetime he was perhaps over-estimated in Europe, if we determine his place in the history of science by the state of science at the end of the nineteenth century. This would, however, be essentially unjust, and most incorrect. The fairer way of putting the case would be, to ask what was he in the middle of the seventeenth century? What would he be, were he living now?

The fact is that he had so many qualities, and pursued so many lines of thought, that they almost dim one another. Whewell remarks of Boyle 'that his disposition led him to suspect all generalities.' From this quality of prudence, and from his steadfast adherence to the supreme test of experiment, he was led to doubt, and to test several opinions in the

abridgment of his philosophical works, and life therein; and the writer in the National Biography.

science of the day, and to overthrow dogmas which had been unquestioned. This scepticism in scientific matters influenced his mind at every moment, and is apparent in many of his treatises on several 'Cosmical' subjects which deeply interested him; but his scientific convictions formed on adequate grounds, and on any subject-matter, were immoveable. It is probable that the greatest service he did to his country and to mankind, was by kindling in the minds of his contemporaries an enthusiasm for science, a desire to explore and know nature, in those turbulent and disastrous days when Wilkins' and Wallis' papers were burnt by the mob, Harvey's anatomical dissections destroyed, and Gresham College turned into barracks. In his day he, more than almost any other man, kept alive the torch which kindled the undying fire of the Royal Society.

The chief writings of Boyle were published as separate treatises from time to time. Most of these volumes, with many manuscripts, exist now in the library of the Royal Society. They were collected into five folio volumes in 1744, and afterwards in six large quarto volumes in 1772, with an elaborate life by the editor, Dr. Birch [1]. This edition contains

---

[1] The life is lengthy, and characteristic of a writer of whom Dr. Johnson said, 'Tom is a lively rogue; he remembers a great deal, and

most of his scientific writings, several theological treatises, and numerous letters from him and to him, many of them highly characteristic of the founders of modern scientific ideas.

To give a detailed account of Boyle's work, its originality, and its effect on Science, even were I equal to the task, cannot be now attempted. Only a general idea can be presented. Following Bacon, he was engaged practically in a revolt against the authority of the Aristotelians and the Schoolmen in respect to the key wherewith to unlock the secrets of the Universe. He accepted to the full the position of enquirer into the smallest details of Nature, and of submitting the facts, where possible, to experiment, instead of assuming principles as the basis for pure deduction. His first, and in some respects most notable and continuous labour, was directed to investigations into the pressure and the elasticity of air. This work resulted in the improvement of the air-pump invented by Guericke, and the establishment of the law often called in the text-books Mariotte's law, though more properly Boyle's law :—namely, that the volume of a gas varies in-

can tell many pleasant stories : but a pen is to Tom a torpedo, the touch of it benumbs his hand and his brain. Tom can talk but cannot write.' Be this as it may, all subsequent writers on Boyle have had to resort to this somewhat unwieldy document, though Birch was not a scientific man.

versely as the pressure if the temperature be constant,
or if the density of the air, or the quantity of it
contained in the same space, is, *caeteris paribus*,
proportional to the pressure it supports. Then
followed, never to be relinquished, studies of the
Chemical and Mechanical constitution of Matter,
and the Laws of Motion, with an eagerness and
ability Celtic to the core. This is consistent, no
doubt, with Herschel's remark ; but with all defer-
ence to Sir J. Herschel, that remark does not seem
to contain the whole truth. Other writers, with
possibly some exaggeration, have spoken of Bacon,
Newton and Boyle as an equal triumvirate. Both
accounts, however, are true in the main. Bacon had
shivered the deductive method as the key to the
knowledge of the Universe ; but in fact his own
remarks in handling his principle are often open to
criticism, and are sometimes even grotesque. Newton,
with whom Boyle was intimate, had first discovered
the widest interpretation of the Laws of Matter
through Astronomy, the most ancient of the sciences.
With his unique power he first showed, passing
beyond Kepler, the method by which the infinite
number of orbs that exist in infinite space are kept
within their appointed bounds, and which of late has
been used by Professor Haughton to illustrate the

motion of molecules and atoms whose dimensions
are so minute that they can scarcely be conceived,
and are still a matter of dispute among competent
mathematicians [1]. Boyle, using a principle of which
more will presently be said, pierced the armour
which concealed the hidden forces and forms of
Nature at any point that was vulnerable. Facts
he felt, rather than knew, would lead to Classifica-
tion and so to the discovery of Law. It is a
certain mark of genius in a man when he is
equally at home with details or with the widest
generalisations. Boyle, by completing his air-pump,
revolutionised the instrumentalities by which the
atmosphere of the earth, the gases, many phenomena
of life, and infinite chemical actions can be for
ever studied. It led, I doubt not, to the suggestion
of rules proposed for the investigation of the
Peak of Teneriffe—no small effort in the seventeenth
century—and thus attempted to settle one physical problem which was set forth with great detail
and precision by the Royal Society of the time.
But he could not do all things. As his intimate
friend Bishop Burnet has told us, it can scarce
be credited what he did. I am not capable of

[1] 1000,000000,000000,000000, or 6000,000000,000000,000000, in a
cubic c. m.

estimating the exact value of some two hundred papers and notes in the ponderous tomes before you, including the 57 in the first 17 volumes of the Philosophical Transactions. I see throughout them the same noble qualities of head and heart. I wish time allowed me to quote if but a few of the great thoughts that crop up like flowers of the spring from the earthy mould of fact in which he delved by day and night, alone or among the congenial spirits of his Invisible College in Oxford, or in London with the Royal Society.

I must commend to those of you who are interested in the historical question of the particular value of any of Boyle's experiments and studies in Chemistry, Mechanics, Physics, Electricity, Matter and Motion in general, Anatomy, Physiology, Medicine, even alleged miracles which seemed to contravene known laws of life, to look into Birch's elaborate life, and the six quarto volumes above referred to, into the three volumes by Shaw containing in convenient form a classified abridgment of his writings, or into the original editions of the special papers which are rarely to be met with.

I will speak now only of three of these papers. Without doubt the long-continued and elaborate experimental work with which his name is most connected in the popular mind is that on the air-pump, which he and Hooke together made a scientific and practical instrument.   His Essays on this are also the best known.   Boyle foresaw the far-reaching results through its agency of a more precise know-ledge of the physical and the chemical properties of the atmosphere, that invisible sea at the bottom of which we live, its relation to all organic life, and to Meteorology in the widest cosmical sense.

Henceforward he applied himself to experiments with this instrument, combined with his increasing power of chemical investigation, into almost all matter, above, upon, and within the Globe : to vapours, to metals and stones of every kind.   He studied respiration in the higher animals, investigated the effects of respired air on Birds, on Reptiles, on Snails, and on Plants, and the manner of death in each.

Though experiments on living animals such as could then be performed were abhorrent to his tender soul, yet the knowledge of Nature was to him a religion ; and he had to pierce through the secrets of life, the cause of disease, of suffering and of death by every means that his ingenuity could devise.

What a joy to him, could he have seen, what we have long suspected, that the all-pervading quality, be it what it may, of electricity, stands in some

B

similar or analogous relation to brain and mental action as air to respiration. It seems clear to our time that we are on the verge of some revelation of this connection, as well as of its relation to light and to heat. He did, indeed, as it was sure he would, seek in various ways, and endeavour to extend the knowledge of Magnetism and Electricity. But the time was not yet come.

I would name also especially his paper on the Natural History of a Country, great and small. It is worth your attention as the first 'Admiralty Manual of Scientific Enquiry': and seeing how precise a thinker and worker Boyle was, this essay is highly characteristic of the universality of his intellect and his interests.

He divides the things to be observed into 'supraterraneous, terrestrial, subterraneous, and otherwise,' but at present, he says, 'into those things that respect the heavens, the air, the water, the earth.' Then follow (1) a few general suggestions as to latitude and longitude, and some astronomical hints ; (2) more precise questions concerning the air, requiring in fact most careful observation as to seasons, weather, winds, meteors, diseases, contagion, constitutions of inhabitants ; (3) suggestions concerning the sea, tides, lakes, rivers, fishes—their store, bigness, goodness, seasons, haunts, peculiarities and the like; (4) the earth, its nature and character, the inhabitants, careful queries concerning these, native or strangers; all the vegetation in detail, and then the subterraneous properties, with great minuteness. In respect of mines, under six heads he proposes ninety separate enquiries, including particulars as to the miners in their various operations and furnaces, the country which surrounds the mines, the natives, the cattle, their diseases, and the traditions of the people.

When you read this short paper you cannot fail to see that the writer, one of the most precise and careful of men, whose habit was to enquire into the smallest details, had ever in his mind at the same time the most general questions affecting the composition and nature of the planet as a whole, with all that is therein.

The third kind of paper which is suggested for your consideration as evidence of Boyle's character is that on MEDICINE.

He makes, first of all, some general and shrewd observations as to the usefulness of Natural Philosophy for the Arts; for, he says, there is a probability that no small improvement may be made in men's proficiency through experimental knowledge of those arts which are the chiefest instruments of man's dominion over the creatures. 'These arts (to divide them, he says, not accurately but popularly) do serve either to relieve man's necessity as physick and husbandry, or for his accommodation, as the trades of shoemakers, dyers, tanners, &c., or for his delight, as the trades of painters, confectioners, perfumers, &c., to all which arts, and many others allied to them, philosophical experiments and observations may by a knowing naturalist be made to extend a meliorating influence,' and himself studied several of them : a hint this to modern councils for technical education.

In another passage he describes a man of fortune and every worldly good, who himself despised Natural Philosophy as did his doctor, who by ignorance or mistake deprived him of all of them.

Then leaving generalities, and saying that he does not pretend to be a doctor, he divides Medicine into Physiological, Pathological, Semeiotical, Hygienical, Therapeutical. As to the Physiological, he says the Physician must take much of his doctrine from the Naturalist; and quotes Aristotle that 'the Naturalist endeth where Medicine begins, and Medicine begins where the Naturalist endeth.' He discusses the value of experiments on the living bodies of men and of animals, condemns vivisections that 'physicians had performed by leave of kings on malefactors; and

scrupled not to destroy man in order to know him.'
He shows how things that cannot be otherwise known
may be learnt by the dissection of dogs, swine, and
other live creatures, and things found that hold good
in human bodies. He himself, that it might not be
pretended that the experiment was unfaithfully
made, assisted in the extirpation of a spleen from
a young setting dog; and 'yet this puppy in less
than a fortnight grew not only well, but became as
sportive as before. He relates a case of successful
extirpation in a woman by an Italian surgeon. He
then discusses, with care but generally, the value of
dissections in the living and the dead of many classes
of animals. Into these I cannot enter now, and
it is clear that modern knowledge supersedes all
older information on these points. At the same
time he performed many experiments similar to
those of the present century, both on the nervous
and circulatory apparatus.

The next essay is Pathological. He insists on the
value of the study of the diseases that occur in
animals by illustrating the nature of some of the
diseases incident to human bodies. It may interest
some here to know that with the then Warden of
Wadham and Mr. Christopher Wren he tried the
effect of introducing 'a warm solution of opium in

sack into the blood-vessel of a dog,' and 'the dog soon
nodding, and being very sleepy, he was whipped about
the garden, and being kept awake and in motion, he
not only recovered but began to grow fat so mani-
festly, that it was admired, and very soon after stolen.'

I must not now pursue the Semeiotical Hygienic
and Therapeutical portions. As to the Hygienic,
he discusses diets, the scientific and chemical mode
of preserving foods, of analyzing water, and air, in
regard to their effect on life. In the latter he insists
that this so useful therapeutical part of physic is
'capable of being much improved by a knowing naturalist, especially if he be an intelligent and expert
chemist.' He makes quaint and caustic remarks on
the inefficiency of physicians for want of natural
philosophy, and suggests various directions in which
chemists and naturalists may help the *materia medica.*
Although many of the hints have, by lapse of time,
become useless, the tone of a scientific observer and
careful experimenter fills every page of the whole
treatise. He considers moreover how to make drugs
cheap as well as efficient—shows that Pharmacy
generally can be greatly improved. He ends this
elaborate essay with some touching comparisons
between the life of a soldier and the duty of Physicians, and says when he considers that the Lord Jesus

'went about doing good, and healing all manner of sickness and all manner of diseases among the people, he cannot but think such an employment worthy of the very noblest of His disciples.'

There is only one weakness in these papers, if weakness it be. He was (it may be said) too much of a Utilitarian, and so far might seem to idealists and ontologists a narrow man. He speaks once somewhat slightingly of Astronomy. It is a strange, but still intelligible paradox. He felt the wonders of Infinity to be beyond his particular grasp. He did not live in the day of Huggins and his fellows. He had not seen the star maps of Isaac Roberts and the other exponents of the overwhelming revelations of the stars, their number, their importance, their circumambient ether, nor had he more than dreamt of the questions now arising as to light and heat, and the hidden energies of the Universe, which the enquiries of the much-lamented Clerk Maxwell, Crookes, or Tesla are beginning to scan, which Lord Kelvin and his brethren are making intelligible to us ordinary men, though he had a keen insight into the 'corpuscular or mechanical' constitution of matter in or out of motion, on which he wrote in minute detail and great comprehensiveness. Yet I would strongly defend this flaw, if flaw it be, and value it as one may value a discord in music, a pause in a rhetorical speech. Are not the Utilities of science as great as the quest after Truth? Are they not, in fact, often discoveries as real as is a Law? What shall we say of Chloroform, of the Telegraph, of Electric Lighting, of Cunarders and Ironclads, of Photographs of the Sky—all of which have arisen in the reign of our present Sovereign by reason of the progress of pure Science and its application? Shall Boyle be blamed that he had a strong belief in the utility of truth and of knowledge for mankind? Bacon himself, in his New Atlantis, wherein he sets forth his ideal of life, looks on research and discovery as of value, not only for their own sake, but for the practical advantage and convenience of the world.

THUS far we have considered the character of Robert Boyle as searcher for truth by Scientific questioning of Nature.

We have now, two centuries later, in the history of Oxford and of the world, to ask, whether we can worthily perpetuate his memory and carry on his work in Physical Science with the same temper of pure reason and the same reverent spirit, availing ourselves of the means which are our possession in these later days.

But before we answer this, there is another side of his life which I do not propose to consider fully, but which it would be wrong to him, unjust to you, and unfair to Modern Science wholly to pass by.

A great part of Boyle's life and much of his writing was devoted to Theological questions. The present state of modern thought, and the very nature of the Institute in which we are assembled, make it absolutely necessary to ask ourselves whether in this respect he is worthy of our regard and admiration, or whether this fact detracts from his character as a scientific man. Be this as it may, it is my belief, that were he with us now, he would be, as he was in the seventeenth century, in the widest sense a theological enquirer, but under the conditions of modern thought and knowledge ; and further, that were it otherwise, he would not fill the place as a scientific man which ought to be filled by a leader of modern thought in Oxford.

It would be tedious to you if I were to attempt to give a full account of his theological essays.

It is certain that from early life, the search after the FIRST CAUSE of the visible and demonstrable in Nature, the question what Nature is, was with Boyle the Problem of Problems. This is recognised in the motto prefixed to the Collected Edition of his

works, *Ex rerum causis supremam noscere causam.*
His pure reason, however, was not led aside, as it
were, by some inherited instinct which tempted him
to worship, as the men of Athens worshipped, 'the
unknown God.' He sought as fully as the most
thoroughgoing Agnostic of the nineteenth century
to grasp the works of Creation with his intellect,
while he loved and put trust in an Author of Nature,
Whom he regarded with a temper as childlike and
simple as the Seers and the Psalmists of Israel. His
interesting and elaborate papers on what is the
meaning of Nature absolutely prove this.

Difficult as is the task, in the short time at my
disposal, a few sentences may be accepted as the key
to the religious mind of Robert Boyle.

His active and powerful intellect was imbued, and
some would say tainted, with the conviction which
was tersely expressed by Sir Thomas Brown: '*Nature
is the Art of God.*' This profound sentiment led him
by every gift he possessed, by every power he had,
to study with the full intensity of his character
all he could learn as of the Art, so of the Artificer,
as of the Law, so of the Law-giver of the Universe.
He saw his own littleness in the immensity of the
Universe ; his instincts drove him to explore it with
boundless energy, but with humble confidence ; and,

having explored so far as possible, to trust and to adore. As he studied, so also he criticised. Yet at every step, like that 'great restorer of Physicks Verulam,' who died the year before Boyle was born, Boyle desired, as did Bacon in his Student's Prayer, 'that human things may not prejudice such as are divine,' and that 'there may be given unto faith the things that are of faith.' In his theological writings Boyle becomes incensed with the Physicists who dogmatised without adequate data and decided without experiment.

He sets forth in two treatises his general opinion as to the nature of the Universe. In the paper on the Excellence and Grounds of the Corpuscular or Mechanical Philosophy he says :—

'I am far from meaning with the Epicureans, that atoms, meeting together by chance in an infinite vacuum, are able of themselves to produce the world and all its phenomena ; nor with some modern philosophers that, supposing God to have put into the whole mass of matter such an invariable quantity of motion, He needed do no more to make the world, the material parts being able by their own unguided motions to cast themselves into systematic order[1].' He then goes on to 'plead only for such a philosophy

---

[1] Boyle's Works, vol. iv. pp. 68-69.

as reaches but to things purely corporeal,' distinguish-
ing ' between the first original of things, and the subsequent course of nature,' and declares his belief
' not only that God gave motion to matter, but that
in the beginning He so guided the various motions of
the parts of it,' as that ' the seminal principles' should
furnish the 'models of living creatures'; and so combined them by rules of motion and order as to form
what we 'call the Laws of Nature.' Then, as to the
sustenance of the universe, he claimed the right 'to
teach, that the universe being once formed by God,'
and the laws of motion being settled by God's
' general providence, the phenomena of the world,
thus constituted, are physically produced by the
mechanical affections of the parts of matter,' and by
their mutual operation 'according to mechanical
laws [1].'

He says, further, that we cannot ' conceive any
principles more primary than matter and motion.
For either both of them were immediately created
by God, or, ... if matter be eternal, motion must
either be produced by some immaterial, supernatural
agent, or it must immediately flow by way of emana-
tion from the nature of the matter it appertains to.'

' Neither,' he says again, ' can there be any phy-

[1] Boyle's Works, vol. iv. p. 70.

sical principles more simple than matter and motion ; neither of them being resoluble into any things whereof they may be . . . said to be composed.'

The whole of the treatise whence these passages are quoted is characteristic of the man, and of the manner of his time.

Of his greatness of mind in relation to the broad standpoint of religion the following may be taken as an instance :—

'In the book of Nature, as in a well-contrived romance, the parts have such a connection and relation to one another, and the things we would discover are so darkly or incompletely knowable by those that precede them, that the mind is never satisfied till it comes to the end of the book [1].'

And again : 'He that reads an excellent book, or sees some rare engine, will be otherwise affected with the sight or the perusal, if he knows it to have been made by a friend or a parent, than if he considers it but as made by a stranger, whom he has no particular reason to be concerned for [2].'

And still more, he shows a breadth of view much to be considered by some in our own day:—

'The study of physics has one prerogative (above that of divinity), which, as it is otherwise a great

---

[1] Boyle's Works, iv. p. 36. [2] Ibid. p. 37.

excellency, so does much add to the delightfulness of it. I mean, the certainty, and clearness, and thence resulting satisfactoriness of our knowledge of physical—in comparison of any we can have of theological—matters, whose being dark and uncertain, the nature of the things themselves, and the numerous controversies of differing sects about them, sufficiently manifest [1].'

Similar passages might be quoted indefinitely.

In THEOLOGY the basis of his faith was laid first in Nature, and secondly in the Scriptures as revealing through the lives and the teaching of men and of nations the supreme principles of conscience, of right and wrong in their bearing on the human race. He never mistrusts his Faith, though always he will put it frankly to the test of his Reason.

It follows, therefore, that since both in Science and in Theology the last two centuries have raised questions and taught many facts of the first importance to man, which in Bacon's time were neither known nor accessible, yet the application of reason and faith respectively to human knowledge and human ignorance in their time and place, remain as then unaltered except in detail. I will go further, and say that the total impression of a long life of observation and

---

[1] Boyle's Works, iv. p. 41.

action on my own mind is, that in the greatest men the two qualities are combined with an intensity not possessed by narrower minds. Is it necessary to name Galileo, Kepler, Newton, the Herschels, Faraday ?

Bishop Burnet, a man of the Court, a shrewd observer of mankind, an outspoken and able writer, and an intimate friend for many years, gives this remarkable account of Boyle, and expresses his own opinion of the effect of Science on the moral nature of man. In his discourse the Bishop says :—

Knowledge opens the mind, and fills it with great notions; the viewing the works of God, even in a general survey, gives, insensibly, a greatness to the soul. But the more extended and exact, the more minute and severe the inquiry is, the soul grows to be thereby the more enlarged, by the variety of observations that is made; either on the great orbs and wheels, that have made their first motion, as well as their law of moving, from the Author of all; or on the composition of bodies, on the regularities, as well as the irregularities of nature; and the mimicry of its heat and motion, that artificial fires do produce and show. This knowledge goes into the history of past times and remote climates; and with those livelier observations on art and nature, which give a pleasant entertainment and amusement to the mind, there are joined, in some, the severer studies, the more laborious, as well as the less pleasant, study of languages, on design to understand the sense, as well as the discoveries, of former ages; and, more particularly, to find out the true sense of the sacred writings.

These are all the several varieties of the most useful parts of knowledge; and these do spread over all the powers of the soul of him that is capable of them, a sort of nobleness, that makes him become, thereby, another kind of creature than otherwise he ever could have been : he has a larger size of soul, and vaster thoughts, that can measure the spheres, and enter into the theories, of the heavenly bodies; that can observe the proportion of lines and numbers, the composition and mixtures of the several sorts of beings. This world, this life, and the mad scene we are in, grow to be but little and inconsiderable things, to one of great views and noble theories ; and he who is upon the true scent of real and useful knowledge has always some great thing or other in prospect : new scenes do open to him, and these draw after them discoveries, which are often made before even those who made them were either aware or in expectation of them : these, by an endless chain, are still pointing at, or leading into, further discoveries. In all these a man feels as sensibly, and distinguishes as plainly, an improvement of the strength and compass of his powers, from the feebleness which ignorance and sloth bring upon them, as a man in health of body can distinguish between the life and strength which accompany it, and the flatness and languidness that disease bring with them. This enlarges a man's empire over the creation, and makes it more entirely subject to him, by the engines it invents to subdue and manage it, by the dissections in which it is more opened to his view, and by the observation of what is profitable or hurtful in every part of it ; from which he is led to correct the one and exalt the other. This leads him into the knowledge of the hidden virtues that are in plants and minerals; this teaches him to purify these from the alloys that are wrapped about them, and to improve them by other mixtures. In a word, this lets a man into the mysteries of nature ; it gives him, both the keys that open it, and a thread, that will lead him further than he durst promise himself at first. We can easily apprehend the surprising joy of one born blind that, after many years of darkness, should be blessed with sight ; and the leaps and life of thought that such a one should feel, upon so ravishing a change : so the new regions into which a true son of knowledge enters ; the new subjects, and the various shapes of them, that do daily present themselves to him, give his mind a flight, a raisedness, and a refined joy, that is of another nature than all the soft and bewitching pleasures of sense. And though the highest reaches of knowledge do more clearly discover the weakness of our shortsighted powers, and show us difficulties that gave us no pain before, because we did not apprehend them ; so that, in this respect, 'he that increases knowledge, increases sorrow' ; yet it is a real pleasure to a searcher after truth to be undeceived, to see how far he can go, and where he must make his stops. It is true, he finds he cannot compass all that he hath proposed to himself ; yet he is both in view of it, and in the way to it ; where he finds so many noble entertainments, that though he cannot find out the whole work of God, which the preacher tells us, that 'though a wise man thinks he may know it, yet, even he, shall not be able to find it out' ; yet he has this real satisfaction in himself, that he has greater notions, nobler views, and finer apprehensions, than he could have ever fallen upon in any other method of life.

His *knowledge* was of so vast an extent, that, if it were not for the variety of vouchers, in their several sorts, I should be afraid to say all I know. He carried the study of the Hebrew very far into the rabbinical writings, and the other oriental

C

languages. He had read so much of the fathers, that he had formed out of it a clear judgment of all the eminent ones. He had read a vast deal on the scriptures, and had gone, very nicely, through the whole controversies of religion; and was a true master in the whole body of divinity. He ran the whole compass of the mathematical sciences; and, though he did not set himself to spring new game, yet he knew even the abstrusest parts of geometry. Geography, in the several parts of it, that related to navigation or travelling: history and books of travels, were his diversions. He went, very nicely, through all the parts of physic; only, the tenderness of his nature made him less able to endure the exactness of anatomical dissections, especially of living animals; though he knew those to be the most instructing: but, for the history of nature, ancient and modern, of the productions of all countries, of the virtues and improvements of plants, of ores and minerals and all the varieties that are in them, in different climates, he was by much, by very much, the readiest and the perfectest I ever knew, in the greatest compass, and with the truest exactness. This put him in the way of making all that vast variety of experiments, beyond any man, as far as we know, that ever lived. And in these, as he made a great progress in new discoveries, so he used so nice a strictness, and delivered them with so scrupulous a truth, that all who have examined them have found how safely the world may depend upon them. But his peculiar and favourite study was chemistry; in which he engaged with none of those ravenous and ambitious designs, that draw many into them. His design was, only, to find out nature; to see into what principles things might be resolved; and of what they were compounded; and to prepare good medicaments for the bodies of men [1].

[1] Burnet's lives, edited by Bishop Jebb, 1833, p. 358.

AND if this brief account of Robert Boyle be true, we may ask, Are the Oxford opportunities conformable to the just desires of your Society? I think that, with all our incompleteness and imperfections, they are. All Scientific progress rests in some degree on what has gone before.

The ground on which this Museum now stands was thirty-five years ago a ploughed field. There were no Practical Laboratories for Students in the University. The only collections were Buckland's, in rooms in the Old Clarendon, the old Ashmolean collection, and Lee's Anatomy in Christ Church. For experimental purposes, so far as Oxford was concerned, Boyle, Wallis, Mayow, Wren, Sydenham, and Harvey, had almost lived in vain, notwithstanding the zeal in the early part of this century of Buckland, Daubeney, Walker, Rigaud, the Duncans, and Kidd.

You have now an Institution, limited indeed, but arranged from the first with a view to extension.

It aimed at setting forth the study of the Kosmos as a whole and in its parts, so as to embrace Mathematics, Physics, Chemistry, Astronomy, Geology, Mineralogy, Zoology, Anatomy—in the widest sense, Human and Comparative—Physiology, Ethnology,

Anthropology, the Evolution—material, psychical, racial of Man—Medicine, for Animals and Man, Pathological, Preventive and Curative, and a Scientific Library rekindling the light and memory of Radcliffe, as you recall to-day the memory and character of Boyle. Small indeed are some of the parts. You *can* enlarge them all or one. You *may* reduce them all to the needs of Technical Schools.

The entrance by which you came in bears marks of the enthusiasm of JOHN RUSKIN and the young pre-Raphaelites who congregated round him here near forty years since — Millais, Dante Rossetti, W. Morris, Holman Hunt, Woolner, Alexander Munro, Collins, Hughes, and Mr. Watts.

These all took a keen interest in making, as far as was in their power, under many adverse circumstances, the future abode of Physical Science in Oxford as beautiful as useful.

Under their inspiration an allegory of the mystery of the Kosmos is delicately engraved in marble over the arch of the entrance.

It was intended to express allegorically the story of life on our globe, material and psychical, its changes in growth and in decay, its evolution, its end.

As you enter the court, on one hand is the

statue of Aristotle, chiefest, widest, first of the An-
cients, who, grasping the material life of the earth,
set forth also the nature, aims, views and aspiration
of the mind of man with the highest methods then
attainable.   On the other, Bacon, who came after
two thousand years to renew the vast study on
fresh lines and lay the foundation of the work,
which Boyle carried on, the Royal Society per-
petuates, and the civilised world accepts.

Opposite them, across the court, over against these
first leaders of thought, are Galileo and Newton.
Need I say why, or describe the work of these two
men, who perhaps above all in the latter centuries
dispersed the gloom of ages, and made visible to
mankind the burning light of a dazzling universe ?

At either corner, Mathematics, Chemistry, Classifi-
cation, suggest their claim to our gratitude, through
Leibnitz, Philosopher and Mathematician ; Priestley,
genius in Chemistry; Linnæus, keen interpreter of
system in Nature.   Besides these seven, eight
other statues of the great ancient and modern
teachers of Natural Law have been already placed
on fifteen of the thirty-three corbels, in the posi-
tions recommended by the Prince Consort.   Euclid,
Oersted, George Stephenson, Watt, are already
there.   Hippocrates, Harvey, Hunter, Sydenham, on

the north-west side, tell of success and failure in promoting the relief of suffering and the prevention of diseases for more than two thousand years. These all stand at the head of Comparative Anatomy and Morphology, thus reminding that *via ad mortem* is part of life history as much as *via ad vitam*. Hippocrates, who founded Philosophic Medicine in the East ; Harvey, who laid bare the secrets of the higher organic life ; Hunter, who first surveyed the whole range of Anatomy, Physiology, Pathology in all living things ; Sydenham, who brought the clearest observation and true clinical experiment to the bed of the sick ;—all these forcibly tell, as Boyle did, that Natural Philosophy as he called it, or Natural Science as we say in the widest sense, gives the clue to the interpretation and knowledge of all life, its mechanisms, and its actions. But alas! Astronomy, Mathematics, Physics, Chemistry, Geology, Biology, still wait for more representatives. It is to be hoped that soon the eighteen remaining places will be filled either by Archimedes, Hipparchus, Copernicus, Kepler, Cuvier, Buckland, Darwin, Boerhaave, Haller, Bichat, Bell, Laennec, Herder, or Prichard, or other carefully chosen representative men ancient and modern, to tell each their special tale of victory wisely won from nature by labour and by love.

The zeal of the pre-Raphaelite period aimed at embodying Science in all its branches by the help of Art. It was intended that each science of the Kosmos should be represented by a statue of its greatest worthy; that a specimen of every natural order should be carved on one of the 192 capitals; and that each one of the 128 columns should be a noble specimen of British rocks. The initial zeal, by which these artistic representations were commemorative and instructive (all due to private munificence, for the University was asked for nothing in this matter), has given way under, shall I say, the practical and utilitarian temper of our day, and, may I dare to add, by reason of a less interest in the broader views of the Universe which have been superseded by devotion to special studies and research, and by a zeal for technical and professional education, as though in our day a sense of the connection of the Physical Sciences and the abiding conviction of the Unity of Nature had not become more than ever a necessity for all specialists who give their lives to the details of a single region of Nature.

In the few words in which I have endeavoured to illustrate the court of the Museum, I have intentionally omitted that portion of the Institution which would interest Boyle, were he still with us, quite

as much as the experimental laboratories of Physics,
Chemistry, Physiology, the Observatory, with its ad-
vanced and subtle modes of astronomical research,—
I mean the illustrations of Anthropology. These, I
believe, would attract him at least as much as those
to which he devoted most of his energies. The great
problems studied by Darwin and by Weissmann, the
modern knowledge of the human race, whether in
corporeal constitution and evolution or in psycho-
logical development, would, with his theological
interests, be now, as formerly, to him the Problem
of Problems. Modern research by modern critics
has in these departments created a new world of
thought. The questions raised by Locke or Berke-
ley, and more or less answered by Kant or Lotze,
and a host of writers on mental and ontological
Science, would be seriously discussed by the man
who looked out on Nature, material and spiritual,
as indissolubly connected, who learned Hebrew
and other Eastern languages to read in their native
tongue the words of the prophets and poets of
the East. He would, with Max Müller and many
others, seriously endeavour to use all the discoveries in
language and in history to solve the problems arising
from consideration of the reason or the soul of man.
Utilitarian as in some sort Boyle was, he would not,

were he still present with us, study man only for the purpose of any one technical though beneficent art. He would pursue the problem of his higher nature by every means in his power, fearlessly, rationally, reverently. He would now be plunged into all the questions of modern thought and criticism, solved and unsolved, as to man's destiny and his relation to the Infinite. These thoughts and inquiries would now as then stimulate him to employ experiment and research in every direction open to him, and with every power which he possessed, and by every means within his reach.

I have endeavoured to justify myself, if justification be necessary, for suggesting the enquiry why now and here, in this day and in this Institute, questions of so-called religious thought arise and are pressed on our attention. The existence of the Pitt-Rivers Collection was purposely left unnoticed, when I began to speak of the range of subjects which we in our age have to consider. It was impossible in a short address to speak of the evolution of the ethical and moral nature in the races of man, of his differentiation from the animals his fellow-tenants of our little planet, and of their differentiation from the myriad unconscious natures which, in some way

yet unknown, are separated from the lowest animal
life, and constitute the vegetable world; or of the
actions of apparent affinity, which make, for instance, certain leucocytes (as they are called) deadly
enemies to invading and dangerous microbes. In
every direction the fringes of the veil are lifting,
yet never, perhaps, to be wholly removed.

Of the problem of life Lord Kelvin says—'The
real phenomena of life infinitely transcend human
science.'

The infinitely great and the infinitely small in
time or space, though often outside the range of direct
experiment, are becoming daily the objects of observation. They are sometimes amenable only to reason
and hypothesis. They leave to Faith the concept of
the Cause of All.

The successors of your President and our hosts
to-night will have the whole range of scientific
thought open to them in selecting those who, under
the Ægis of Boyle, experimenter and divine, shall
expound in this place their portion of the Kosmos.
They may range through all the realms of knowledge
from microbes to man; from the infinitesimally small
to the infinitely great; from the action of inferred
atoms to the movements and composition of immeasur-
able orbs; from the certainties of demonstrable facts

in our little world to the problems or probabilities of countless invisible planets, rolling their way round suns as yet undiscovered, outside and beyond the more than hundred millions that are now appreciable by our limited faculties of assisted sight.

Mr. President, some colleagues whom I loved, and who helped to lay the foundations on which you can build, have ceased from their labours. They who are now with you all have our respect, our regard, our support. In their respective laboratories for Astronomy, Physics, Chemistry, Morphology, Zoology, Anatomy, Physiology, Anthropology, Geology, and in the Radcliffe Library, you have opportunities which Boyle could not have and Bacon could only dream.

May many of your Society that has rekindled the light and the memory of Robert Boyle in Oxford, follow him from Oxford to London, and treading in his footsteps join hereafter the great Society of which he was one of the chiefest founders.

For many years to come may the youth of Oxford have yearly presented to them and their friends through a Boyle Lecture which they have founded, some progressive aspect of truth in regard to the Kosmos by a true representative of the intellect, knowledge and character of Robert Boyle—by a master mind which, while seeking to grasp a truth of the Universe, is neither lost in the weary mazes of ontological speculation, nor dwarfed by the exclusive study of some special details of the infinite and incomprehensible Universe.

If I have dwelt on the theological side of Boyle's character, it has been because it is the side which some may now consider to be a weakness. It was to him a source of strength. It shows, moreover, conclusively that the most profound belief in Divine goodness and power is not only consistent with, but is an incentive to, the most intense and strictly scientific study of phenomena, their interpretation and their laws, as presented in the so-called material universe.

'When we view the world,' says Lotze[1], 'as a whole, we see everywhere wonders and poetry, and recognize that it is only limited and one-sided apprehensions of particular departments of the finite that are prose. But to this we would add that it is the business of men not to take the name of these wonders and this poetry in vain, and to revel in continual contemplation of them, but above all things to cultivate that more modest realm of scientific knowledge which is able, not, indeed, to lead us into the pro-

---

[1] Lotze, Microcosmus, 3rd ed. vol. ii. p. 720.

mised land, but to keep us from wandering too far out of the road that leads to it.'

The attitude of Robert Boyle in pursuit of truth in the two great subjects which filled his mind may be summed up in well-known words of our great living poet :—

> Let knowledge grow from more to more,
> But more of reverence in us dwell.
>
> We have but Faith : we cannot know ;
> For knowledge is of things we see ;
> And yet we trust it comes from Thee,
> A beam in darkness : let it grow.

www.ingramcontent.com/pod-product-compliance
Lightning Source LLC
Chambersburg PA
CBHW032139080426
42733CB00008B/1130